Faithful ROADS

A JOURNEY OF PRAYER THROUGH LIFE'S CHANGES

BY: CHAZ TERRY

Why a Devotional Matters

A devotional is a book designed to guide you in your daily spiritual journey. It provides you with reflections, prayers, and scriptures that help deepen your connection with God. For new adults, the transition into adulthood brings many challenges and uncertainties. This devotional is crafted to help you navigate this critical phase of life by making prayer a priority. Through these pages, you'll discover why prayer is essential and how it can positively transform your life. Each chapter will guide you through specific aspects of prayer, offering practical advice and spiritual insights. This book will show you how to invite God into every area of your life through prayer, and why this is vital to your journey as a new adult.

Contents

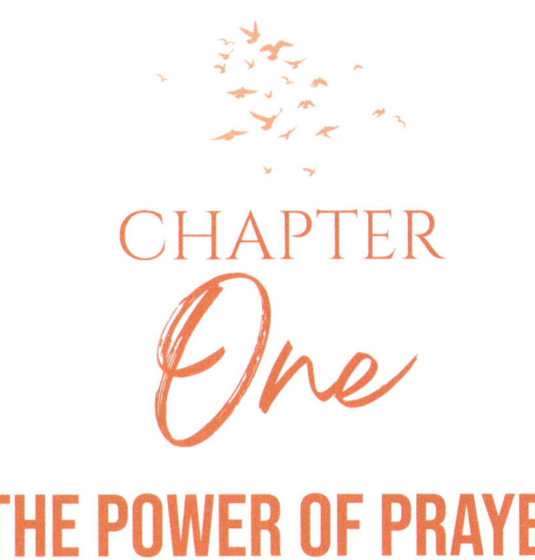

CHAPTER
One

THE POWER OF PRAYER

Prayer is more than just a religious ritual; it is a lifeline, a direct line of communication with God. For new adults, learning to prioritize prayer is essential as you navigate the many changes and challenges that come with this stage of life. Prayer is where you find strength when you are weak, guidance when you are lost, and comfort when you are hurting. The Bible reminds us in Philippians 4:6-7, "Be careful for nothing; but in everything by prayer and supplication with thanksgiving let your requests be made known unto God. And the peace of God, which passeth all understanding, shall keep your hearts and minds through Christ Jesus."

Through prayer, we align our hearts with God's will and invite His presence into our daily lives. It's in these quiet moments with God that we can lay down our burdens and trust Him to provide for our needs. "Cast thy burden upon the Lord, and he shall sustain thee: he shall never suffer the righteous to be moved" (Psalm 55:22, KJV).

As you journey through this devotional, you will find that prayer is not just a way to ask for what you need, but also a way to grow closer to God, to understand His heart, and to allow His peace to fill your life. With each chapter, you'll be encouraged to reflect on different aspects of prayer and how they can impact your life as a new adult. Remember, prayer is a powerful tool that can change not only your circumstances but also your perspective.

EMBRACING NEW BEGINNINGS

Stepping into a new season of life can be both exhilarating and daunting. Whether you're starting a new job, moving to a new place, or entering a new relationship, the unknowns can often lead to feelings of anxiety or uncertainty. During these times, prayer becomes an essential anchor, grounding us in the unchanging promises of God. As it is written, "Behold, I will do a new thing; now it shall spring forth; shall ye not know it? I will even make a way in the wilderness, and rivers in the desert" (Isaiah 43:19, KJV). This verse reassures us that God is always at work, creating new paths and opportunities even when we feel lost or uncertain.

In moments of change, it's important to remember the wisdom of Proverbs 3:5-6, which advises us to "Trust in the Lord with all thine heart; and lean not unto thine own understanding. In all thy ways acknowledge him, and he shall direct thy paths." Trusting God with our future requires us to relinquish control, acknowledging that He sees the bigger picture when we cannot. Through prayer, we express our trust in God's plan and invite Him to guide us through the challenges ahead.

Prayer also reminds us of God's unchanging nature, even when everything around us seems to be shifting. Hebrews 13:8 tells us, "Jesus Christ the same yesterday, and today, and forever." No matter what new situations arise, God's character remains constant. He is always faithful, always present, and always ready to guide us through every new beginning.

Before moving forward, take a moment to pray: "Heavenly Father, I come to You with an open heart, ready to embrace the new opportunities You have placed before me. I pray for Your wisdom to make the right decisions and for Your peace to calm any anxieties I may have. Lead me, Lord, in the direction You want me to go, and help me to trust that You are with me every step of the way. Thank You for Your constant presence and unfailing love. In Jesus' name, Amen."

Think about the changes you are currently experiencing. How can you include God in these new beginnings? Consider writing down a prayer that speaks to your situation, asking for God's guidance and peace as you move forward. Reflect on how these Bible verses can be a source of comfort and encouragement, reminding you of God's presence in every new venture.

Prayer is essential as you embrace new beginnings because it aligns your path with God's will and provides the strength to navigate the unknown. By making prayer a priority in your life, you invite God to be an active part of your journey, guiding you every step of the way.

Notes

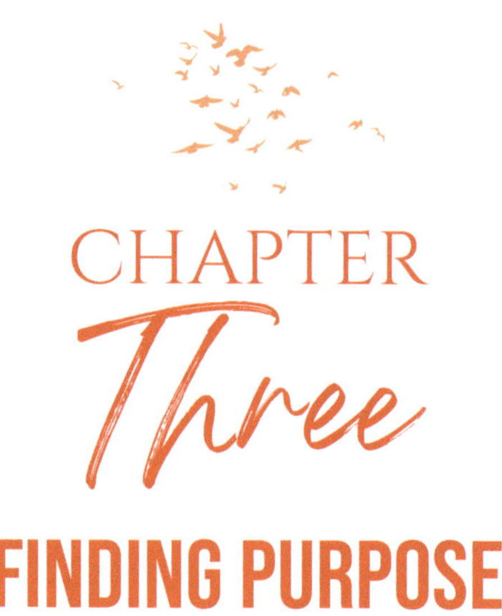

CHAPTER Three

FINDING PURPOSE

Discovering your purpose is a journey that can bring immense fulfillment and direction to your life. As a new adult, you may find yourself questioning your path, seeking meaning in your career, relationships, and personal aspirations. Prayer plays a crucial role in this discovery, helping you align your desires with God's divine plan. The Bible encourages us in Jeremiah 29:11, "For I know the thoughts that I think toward you, saith the Lord, thoughts of peace, and not of evil, to give you an expected end" (Jeremiah 29:11, KJV). This assurance reminds us that God has a specific purpose for each of us, filled with hope and a future.

In your quest to find purpose, it's essential to seek God's guidance. Proverbs 16:3 advises, "Commit thy works unto the Lord, and thy thoughts shall be established" (Proverbs 16:3, KJV). By dedicating your plans and ambitions to Him, you invite His wisdom and direction into every aspect of your life. Prayer becomes the medium through which you communicate your desires and listen for His voice, helping you discern the path He has set for you.

Additionally, seeking purpose often involves overcoming doubts and fears. Philippians 1:6 reassures us, "Being confident of this very thing, that he which hath begun a good work in you will perform it until the day of Jesus Christ" (Philippians 1:6, KJV). Trusting that God is actively working in your life provides the confidence needed to pursue your calling with perseverance and faith.

Before moving forward, take a moment to pray: "Heavenly Father, I thank You for the purpose You have for my life. Help me to seek Your will in all that I do and to trust in Your perfect plan. Guide me in making decisions that honor You and fulfill the destiny You have prepared for me. Fill me with Your Holy Spirit, that I may walk confidently in the path You have set before me. In Jesus' name, Amen."

Reflect on the areas of your life where you feel called to make a difference. How can you use your unique abilities and passions to serve God and others? Write down your thoughts and prayers, asking God to illuminate the way forward and to provide the strength and courage needed to pursue your purpose.

Prayer is instrumental in finding purpose because it aligns our hearts with God's will and opens us to His divine guidance. By making prayer a priority, you allow God to shape your journey, ensuring that your actions and decisions are in harmony with His greater plan. This alignment not only brings clarity and direction but also instills a sense of peace and assurance, knowing that you are fulfilling the purpose He has designed for you.

Notes

BUILDING STRONG RELATIONSHIPS

Relationships are an essential part of our lives, providing support, companionship, and growth. As a new adult, building strong, healthy relationships is crucial, whether they are friendships, family connections, or romantic partnerships. Prayer is a powerful tool in cultivating these relationships, helping you to foster love, understanding, and forgiveness. The Bible reminds us in Ecclesiastes 4:9-10, "Two are better than one; because they have a good reward for their labour. For if they fall, the one will lift up his fellow: but woe to him that is alone when he falleth; for he hath not another to help him up" (Ecclesiastes 4:9-10, KJV). This scripture highlights the importance of companionship and the strength that comes from being in supportive relationships.

When it comes to building strong relationships, prayer should be at the foundation. By praying for those you care about, you invite God's presence into your interactions, seeking His guidance on how to nurture these connections. Colossians 3:13 encourages us to "Forbear one another, and forgive one another, if any man have a quarrel against any: even as Christ forgave you, so also do ye" (Colossians 3:13, KJV). Through prayer, you can ask for the grace to be patient, to forgive, and to love others as Christ loves you.

Prayer also helps us to recognize when relationships are not healthy or when boundaries need to be established. Proverbs 27:17 teaches, "Iron sharpeneth iron; so a man sharpeneth the countenance of his friend" (Proverbs 27:17, KJV). True friends and partners should help you grow and become better versions of yourselves. Through prayer, you can seek God's wisdom on which relationships to invest in and how to maintain healthy boundaries.

Before moving forward, take a moment to pray: "Heavenly Father, I ask for Your wisdom and guidance in all my relationships. Help me to build connections that honor You and bring out the best in both myself and others. Teach me to love selflessly and to support those around me with a Christ-like spirit. Protect me from relationships that may lead me astray and guide me towards those that strengthen my walk with You. In Jesus' name, Amen."

Reflect on the relationships in your life. How can you be more intentional about praying for the people you care about? Consider how your prayers can positively impact these connections, bringing about healing, growth, and deeper understanding. Write down specific prayers for your relationships and trust that God will work through them to bring about His will.

Prayer is essential in building strong relationships because it centers them on God's love and wisdom. By making prayer a priority in your interactions, you open the door for God to work in your relationships, bringing about transformation, healing, and growth. Strong relationships rooted in prayer are not only more resilient but also more fulfilling, as they reflect the love and grace of God.

Notes

CHAPTER
Five

OVERCOMING FEAR AND ANXIETY

Fear and anxiety are common struggles that can affect anyone, especially during times of transition or uncertainty. As a new adult, you might face challenges that seem overwhelming, causing stress and worry. Prayer is a powerful way to combat these feelings, bringing peace and reassurance through God's presence. The Bible offers comfort in Philippians 4:6-7, "Be careful for nothing; but in everything by prayer and supplication with thanksgiving let your requests be made known unto God. And the peace of God, which passeth all understanding, shall keep your hearts and minds through Christ Jesus" (Philippians 4:6-7, KJV). This verse encourages us to turn to prayer when we feel anxious, trusting that God's peace will calm our hearts and minds.

When faced with fear, it's important to remember that God is with us, no matter the circumstances. Isaiah 41:10 assures us, "Fear thou not; for I am with thee: be not dismayed; for I am thy God: I will strengthen thee; yea, I will help thee; yea, I will uphold thee with the right hand of my righteousness" (Isaiah 41:10, KJV). Through prayer, we can invite God's strength and protection into our lives, knowing that He will uphold us even in the most challenging situations.

Additionally, 1 Peter 5:7 reminds us to "Cast all your care upon him; for he careth for you" (1 Peter 5:7, KJV). This verse emphasizes that God cares deeply about our struggles and anxieties, and He invites us to lay them at His feet through prayer. By doing so, we release the burden of fear and allow God to carry it for us.

Before moving forward, take a moment to pray: "Heavenly Father, I come before You with the fears and anxieties that weigh heavy on my heart. I ask for Your peace that surpasses all understanding to fill my mind and soul. Help me to trust in Your promises and to cast all my worries upon You. Strengthen me, Lord, and remind me that You are always with me, guiding and protecting me through every trial. In Jesus' name, Amen."

Reflect on the areas of your life where fear and anxiety have taken hold. How can you use prayer to release these burdens to God? Consider writing down your fears and worries, and then offer them up to God in prayer, trusting that He will provide the peace and strength you need.

Prayer is essential in overcoming fear and anxiety because it shifts our focus from our problems to God's power and love. By making prayer a priority, you allow God's peace to guard your heart and mind, freeing you from the grip of fear and allowing you to walk confidently in His protection and care.

Notes

MANAGING FINANCES WITH FAITH

Managing finances is a critical aspect of adult life, and it can often be a source of stress and worry. As a new adult, you may be navigating student loans, budgeting, or planning for future financial goals. It's easy to become overwhelmed by responsibility, but prayer can provide the guidance and peace you need to manage your finances with faith. Proverbs 3:9-10 encourages us, "Honour the Lord with thy substance, and with the firstfruits of all thine increase: So shall thy barns be filled with plenty, and thy presses shall burst out with new wine" (Proverbs 3:9-10, KJV). This scripture reminds us that when we honor God with our finances, He blesses us in return.

Prayer is vital when making financial decisions, as it helps us seek God's wisdom and direction. James 1:5 tells us, "If any of you lack wisdom, let him ask of God, that giveth to all men liberally, and upbraideth not; and it shall be given him" (James 1:5, KJV). By turning to God in prayer, we can gain the insight needed to make sound financial choices, whether it's about saving, spending, or giving.

Furthermore, Philippians 4:19 reassures us that "My God shall supply all your need according to his riches in glory by Christ Jesus" (Philippians 4:19, KJV). This verse serves as a reminder that God is our provider, and we can trust Him to meet our needs as we manage our resources responsibly.

Before moving forward, take a moment to pray: "Heavenly Father, I lift up my finances to You. I ask for Your wisdom in managing the resources You have entrusted to me. Help me to honor You with my financial decisions, to be a good steward of what I have, and to trust in Your provision. Guide me in making choices that align with Your will, and grant me peace as I navigate my financial responsibilities. In Jesus' name, Amen."

Reflect on your current financial situation. How can you incorporate prayer into your financial planning and decision-making? Consider setting aside time to pray specifically about your finances, asking God for guidance and trusting in His provision for your needs.

Prayer is essential in managing finances with faith because it centers our financial decisions on God's wisdom and provision. By making prayer a priority in your financial life, you invite God to lead you in your stewardship, ensuring that your resources are used wisely and in accordance with His will.

CHAPTER
Seven

BALANCING WORK AND REST

In today's fast-paced world, finding a balance between work and rest can be challenging. As a new adult, you may feel the pressure to excel in your career, manage responsibilities, and stay productive, often at the expense of rest. However, God calls us to a life of balance, where work and rest are both valued and necessary. The Bible reminds us in Ecclesiastes 3:1, "To every thing there is a season, and a time to every purpose under the heaven" (Ecclesiastes 3:1, KJV). This verse emphasizes the importance of recognizing the appropriate time for work and the equally important time for rest.

Prayer plays a vital role in helping us find this balance. Through prayer, we can seek God's guidance on how to manage our time and responsibilities effectively. Psalm 127:2 reminds us, "It is vain for you to rise up early, to sit up late, to eat the bread of sorrows: for so he giveth his beloved sleep" (Psalm 127:2, KJV). This scripture highlights the futility of overworking and the value God places on rest. When we pray, we can ask God to help us prioritize our tasks and recognize when it's time to rest, trusting that He will take care of what remains undone.

Furthermore, Jesus Himself set an example of balancing work and rest. In Mark 6:31, He said to His disciples, "Come ye yourselves apart into a desert place, and rest a while" (Mark 6:31, KJV). Even in the midst of ministry, Jesus understood the necessity of stepping away to rest and recharge. Following His example, we too can seek moments of rest through prayer, finding peace and renewal in God's presence.

Before moving forward, take a moment to pray: "Heavenly Father, I thank You for the work You have given me to do, and I ask for Your wisdom in managing my time and responsibilities. Help me to find the right balance between work and rest, to honor You in my labor, and to trust You in my rest. Grant me the peace to step away when needed and the strength to accomplish the tasks before me. May my life reflect the balance that You desire for me, and may I find true rest in You. In Jesus' name, Amen."

Reflect on your current work and rest habits. How can you adjust your routine to better align with the balance God desires for you? Consider setting aside specific times for prayerful rest, trusting that God will bless your work when you honor the need for rest.

Prayer is essential in balancing work and rest because it helps us to align our priorities with God's will, ensuring that we live a life that honors Him in both our labor and our rest. By making prayer a priority, you invite God to guide you in managing your time, leading to a more fulfilling and balanced life.

Notes

CHAPTER *Eight*

DEALING WITH DISAPPOINTMENT

Disappointment is an inevitable part of life. As a new adult, you might face setbacks or unmet expectations in your career, relationships, or personal goals. These moments can be challenging, but they also offer an opportunity to draw closer to God through prayer. The Bible reminds us in Psalm 34:18, "The Lord is nigh unto them that are of a broken heart; and saveth such as be of a contrite spirit" (Psalm 34:18, KJV). This verse reassures us that God is close to us in our pain, offering comfort and healing when we are disappointed.

Prayer is crucial in times of disappointment because it allows us to express our frustrations, hurts, and questions to God. In 1 Peter 5:7, we are encouraged to "Cast all your care upon him; for he careth for you" (1 Peter 5:7, KJV). Through prayer, we can release our burdens to God, knowing that He cares deeply for us and is ready to carry our sorrows.

Moreover, Romans 8:28 reminds us of God's sovereign control over our lives: "And we know that all things work together for good to them that love God, to them who are the called according to his purpose" (Romans 8:28, KJV). Even in disappointment, God is working for our good, shaping our character and faith through the trials we face. Prayer helps us to trust in His plan, even when our circumstances don't make sense.

Before moving forward, take a moment to pray: "Heavenly Father, I come to You with the disappointments and hurts that weigh heavy on my heart. I ask for Your comfort and peace to fill my soul. Help me to trust in Your plan, even when it differs from my own expectations. Give me the strength to persevere through these challenges, knowing that You are with me every step of the way. Turn my disappointments into opportunities for growth and deeper faith. In Jesus' name, Amen."

Reflect on a recent disappointment in your life. How can you bring this situation to God in prayer? Consider writing down your thoughts and feelings, and then release them to God, trusting that He will bring good out of your circumstances.

Prayer is essential in dealing with disappointment because it shifts our focus from the pain of the moment to the greater purpose God has for us. By making prayer a priority, you invite God to transform your disappointments into opportunities for growth and to provide the peace and strength needed to move forward.

Notes

CHAPTER *Nine*

CULTIVATING GRATITUDE

Gratitude is a powerful attitude that can transform our perspective on life. As a new adult, it's easy to become consumed by the challenges and pressures of daily life, but cultivating a heart of gratitude helps us to focus on the blessings God has given us. The Bible encourages us in 1 Thessalonians 5:18, "In everything give thanks: for this is the will of God in Christ Jesus concerning you" (1 Thessalonians 5:18, KJV). This verse reminds us that gratitude is not just an occasional practice but a constant attitude that aligns us with God's will.

Prayer plays a significant role in cultivating gratitude. When we take time to thank God for His blessings, we acknowledge His goodness and faithfulness in our lives. Psalm 100:4 urges us to "Enter into his gates with thanksgiving, and into his courts with praise: be thankful unto him, and bless his name" (Psalm 100:4, KJV). Through prayer, we can develop a habit of gratitude, which opens our hearts to God's presence and deepens our relationship with Him.

Gratitude also shifts our focus from what we lack to what we have. Philippians 4:6-7 reminds us to "Be careful for nothing; but in every thing by prayer and supplication with thanksgiving let your requests be made known unto God. And the peace of God, which passeth all understanding, shall keep your hearts and minds through Christ Jesus" (Philippians 4:6-7, KJV). By combining our requests with thanksgiving, we find peace, knowing that God is in control and that He provides for our every need.

Before moving forward, take a moment to pray: "Heavenly Father, I thank You for the countless blessings You have poured into my life. Help me to cultivate a heart of gratitude, to see Your hand in every situation, and to give thanks in all circumstances. Teach me to focus on Your goodness and to trust in Your provision, even when life is challenging. May my life be a testimony of Your faithfulness and love. In Jesus' name, Amen."

Reflect on the blessings in your life, both big and small. How can you incorporate gratitude into your daily prayers? Consider keeping a gratitude journal where you write down things you are thankful for each day, and use this practice to deepen your prayer life.

Prayer is essential in cultivating gratitude because it centers our hearts on God's goodness and reminds us of His faithfulness. By making prayer a priority, you invite God to fill your life with peace and joy, transforming your outlook and strengthening your relationship with Him.

Notes

CHAPTER

Ten

SEEKING GUIDANCE

Life is full of decisions, both big and small, and as a new adult, you may often find yourself at crossroads, unsure of which path to take. Seeking guidance from God through prayer is crucial in these moments, as it helps you to align your choices with His will. The Bible assures us in Proverbs 3:5-6, "Trust in the Lord with all thine heart; and lean not unto thine own understanding. In all thy ways acknowledge him, and he shall direct thy paths" (Proverbs 3:5-6, KJV). This verse encourages us to trust in God's wisdom rather than relying solely on our own understanding, knowing that He will guide us on the right path.

Prayer is a powerful way to seek God's guidance, especially when facing important decisions. James 1:5 promises, "If any of you lack wisdom, let him ask of God, that giveth to all men liberally, and upbraideth not; and it shall be given him" (James 1:5, KJV). When you pray for wisdom, you invite God to illuminate your path, giving you the clarity and discernment needed to make choices that honor Him.

Moreover, Psalm 32:8 provides further reassurance: "I will instruct thee and teach thee in the way which thou shalt go: I will guide thee with mine eye" (Psalm 32:8, KJV). God's promise to instruct and guide us is a comforting reminder that we are never alone in our decision-making processes. Through prayer, we can seek His direction and trust that He will lead us according to His perfect will.

Before moving forward, take a moment to pray: "Heavenly Father, I seek Your guidance in the decisions I face. I ask for Your wisdom to choose the path that aligns with Your will for my life. Help me to trust in Your direction, even when it's unclear to me. Lead me by Your Spirit, and grant me the discernment to make choices that honor You. Thank You for always being with me and for guiding me with Your unfailing love. In Jesus' name, Amen."

Reflect on any decisions you are currently facing. How can you seek God's guidance through prayer? Consider spending time in quiet reflection, asking God for wisdom and listening for His voice as you discern the steps you should take.

Prayer is essential in seeking guidance because it connects us with God's wisdom and direction. By making prayer a priority in your decision-making, you invite God to lead you on a path that is aligned with His will, ensuring that your choices are grounded in His truth and love.

Notes

CHAPTER
Eleven

EMBRACING FAITH OVER DOUBT

Doubt is something everyone encounters at some point in their spiritual journey, and as a new adult, you may find yourself questioning your faith or struggling with uncertainties. Embracing faith over doubt is not about ignoring your questions but about trusting in God despite them. The Bible teaches us in Hebrews 11:1, "Now faith is the substance of things hoped for, the evidence of things not seen" (Hebrews 11:1, KJV). This verse reminds us that faith is trusting in what we cannot see, believing in God's promises even when they are not immediately visible.

When doubt arises, prayer becomes a powerful tool to strengthen our faith. James 1:6 encourages us, "But let him ask in faith, nothing wavering. For he that wavereth is like a wave of the sea driven with the wind and tossed" (James 1:6, KJV). Through prayer, we can ask God to help us overcome our doubts, to give us the strength to stand firm in our faith, and to trust in His unwavering truth.

Additionally, Mark 9:24 provides a heartfelt example of how to bring our doubts before God: "And straightway the father of the child cried out, and said with tears, Lord, I believe; help thou mine unbelief" (Mark 9:24, KJV). This honest prayer acknowledges the struggle between faith and doubt, asking God to fill the gaps in our belief. It's a reminder that we don't have to have perfect faith; we just need to be willing to bring our doubts to God.

Before moving forward, take a moment to pray: "Heavenly Father, I come to You with the doubts and questions that weigh on my heart. I ask for Your help in strengthening my faith, to trust in Your promises even when I cannot see the way forward. Help me to overcome my unbelief and to rest in the assurance of Your love and truth. Guide me through my uncertainties, and let my faith be a testimony of Your grace and power. In Jesus' name, Amen."

Reflect on any doubts or uncertainties you may be facing. How can you bring these to God in prayer? Consider writing down your doubts and then lifting them up to God, asking Him to help you embrace faith over doubt.

Prayer is essential in embracing faith over doubt because it allows us to connect with God in our moments of uncertainty, trusting that He will strengthen our belief and guide us through our questions. By making prayer a priority, you invite God to work in your life, transforming your doubts into deeper faith and trust in Him.

NAVIGATING DIFFICULT DECISIONS

*L*ife is filled with decisions that can be challenging to navigate, especially when the stakes are high or when the right choice isn't immediately clear. As a new adult, you might face decisions that impact your career, relationships, or personal growth. In these moments, turning to God in prayer is crucial, as it helps you seek His wisdom and peace. The Bible encourages us in Proverbs 16:9, "A man's heart deviseth his way: but the Lord directeth his steps" (Proverbs 16:9, KJV). This verse reminds us that while we may plan our path, it is ultimately God who guides our steps.

Prayer is vital when making difficult decisions because it aligns our desires with God's will. Philippians 4:6-7 offers comfort in these times: "Be careful for nothing; but in every thing by prayer and supplication with thanksgiving let your requests be made known unto God. And the peace of God, which passeth all understanding, shall keep your hearts and minds through Christ Jesus" (Philippians 4:6-7, KJV). Through prayer, we can present our concerns to God, asking for His guidance and trusting that He will provide the peace that surpasses all understanding.

In addition, Proverbs 3:5-6 gives further direction: "Trust in the Lord with all thine heart; and lean not unto thine own understanding. In all thy ways acknowledge him, and he shall direct thy paths" (Proverbs 3:5-6, KJV). Trusting in God's wisdom rather than our own understanding is essential when facing difficult decisions. By seeking His guidance through prayer, we can be confident that He will direct our paths and lead us to the best outcome.

Before moving forward, take a moment to pray: "Heavenly Father, I seek Your wisdom and guidance as I face difficult decisions. Help me to trust in Your plan and to surrender my desires to Your will. Grant me the clarity to see the path You have set before me and the courage to follow it. I ask for Your peace to guard my heart and mind as I navigate these choices, knowing that You are with me every step of the way. In Jesus' name, Amen."

Reflect on any difficult decisions you are currently facing. How can you seek God's guidance through prayer? Consider spending time in prayer, asking God for wisdom and direction, and trusting that He will lead you to the right decision.

Prayer is essential in navigating difficult decisions because it connects us with God's wisdom and peace, ensuring that our choices align with His will. By making prayer a priority, you invite God to guide you through life's challenges, leading you to outcomes that honor Him and bring about His best for your life.

Notes

CHAPTER
Thirteen
PRAYING FOR OTHERS

Intercessory prayer, or praying for others, is a powerful way to express love and compassion. As a new adult, you may often encounter friends, family members, or even strangers who are in need of prayer. By lifting others up in prayer, you not only support them in their struggles but also strengthen your own spiritual life. The Bible encourages us in James 5:16, "Confess your faults one to another, and pray one for another, that ye may be healed. The effectual fervent prayer of a righteous man availeth much" (James 5:16, KJV). This verse highlights the impact of sincere prayer, emphasizing that our prayers for others can bring about powerful results.

When we pray for others, we are following the example set by Jesus, who often prayed for those around Him. In John 17:9, Jesus prays for His disciples, saying, "I pray for them: I pray not for the world, but for them which thou hast given me; for they are thine" (John 17:9, KJV). This demonstrates the importance of interceding for those God has placed in our lives, trusting that our prayers will have a positive impact on their circumstances.

Furthermore, 1 Timothy 2:1 urges us to make intercession a regular part of our prayer life: "I exhort therefore, that, first of all, supplications, prayers, intercessions, and giving of thanks, be made for all men" (1 Timothy 2:1, KJV). By praying for others, we participate in

God's work in their lives, asking Him to intervene, heal, guide, and bless them according to His will.

Before moving forward, take a moment to pray: "Heavenly Father, I lift up those in my life who are in need of Your love and care. I ask that You intervene in their situations, bringing healing, comfort, and guidance where it is needed. Help me to be faithful in praying for others, trusting that You hear and answer my prayers according to Your perfect will. Use me as a vessel of Your love and compassion, and let my prayers be a source of strength and encouragement to those around me. In Jesus' name, Amen."

Reflect on the people in your life who could benefit from your prayers. How can you be more intentional in praying for them? Consider setting aside time each day to pray specifically for others, asking God to meet their needs and to work in their lives in powerful ways.

Prayer is essential in supporting others because it connects us with God's power and love, enabling us to intercede on behalf of those we care about. By making prayer a priority, you become an instrument of God's grace and mercy, helping to bring about His will in the lives of others.

Notes

CHAPTER
Fourteen
SUSTAINING SPIRITUAL GROWTH

Spiritual growth is an ongoing journey that requires commitment, discipline, and, most importantly, a deep connection with God through prayer. As a new adult, you may find yourself navigating new challenges and responsibilities that can either foster or hinder your spiritual development. Maintaining a strong and vibrant relationship with God is crucial for sustaining spiritual growth, and prayer is the foundation upon which this relationship is built. The Bible reminds us in Colossians 2:6-7, "As ye have therefore received Christ Jesus the Lord, so walk ye in him: Rooted and built up in him, and stablished in the faith, as ye have been taught, abounding therein with thanksgiving" (Colossians 2:6-7, KJV). This passage encourages us to be deeply rooted in our faith, growing stronger as we continue our walk with Christ.

Prayer is essential for spiritual growth because it keeps us connected to God, allowing His Spirit to work in us and through us. John 15:5 illustrates this truth: "I am the vine, ye are the branches: He that abideth in me, and I in him, the same bringeth forth much fruit: for without me ye can do nothing" (John 15:5, KJV). Just as branches draw life from the vine, we must draw our spiritual strength from our relationship with Christ through prayer. Without this connection, our spiritual lives can wither and become unfruitful.

Additionally, 2 Peter 3:18 urges us to continue growing in our faith: "But grow in grace, and in the knowledge of our Lord and Saviour Jesus Christ. To him be glory both now and for ever. Amen" (2 Peter 3:18, KJV). Prayer helps us to grow in grace and knowledge by keeping us attuned to God's voice, His teachings, and His guidance. It is through regular, heartfelt prayer that we become more like Christ and more deeply rooted in our faith.

Before moving forward, take a moment to pray: "Heavenly Father, I thank You for the gift of salvation and for the opportunity to grow in my relationship with You. Help me to remain steadfast in my spiritual journey, to seek You daily in prayer, and to be rooted and built up in Your love and truth. Guide me as I continue to grow in grace and knowledge, and let my life be a reflection of Your goodness and glory. Strengthen my faith, Lord, and help me to bear fruit that honors You. In Jesus' name, Amen."

Reflect on your spiritual journey. How can you be more intentional in sustaining your spiritual growth through prayer? Consider setting specific goals for your prayer life, such as dedicating more time to prayer, studying the Bible, or joining a prayer group to encourage consistent spiritual growth.

Prayer is essential in sustaining spiritual growth because it keeps us connected to God, allowing His Spirit to nurture and strengthen our faith. By making prayer a priority, you ensure that your spiritual life remains vibrant and fruitful, grounded in God's love and truth.

CHAPTER
Fifteen
FINDING JOY IN SERVICE

Serving others is a powerful way to reflect God's love and grow in your faith. As a new adult, you may be exploring how you can make a difference in your community, workplace, or even within your own family. Finding joy in service is about recognizing that serving others is not just a duty but a privilege that brings fulfillment and draws you closer to God. The Bible teaches us in Galatians 5:13, "For, brethren, ye have been called unto liberty; only use not liberty for an occasion to the flesh, but by love serve one another" (Galatians 5:13, KJV). This verse reminds us that our freedom in Christ is an opportunity to serve others in love, following the example set by Jesus.

Prayer is vital in cultivating a heart for service. By praying, we seek God's guidance on how best to serve those around us and ask for the strength and compassion needed to serve selflessly. Mark 10:45 emphasizes the example of Christ: "For even the Son of man came not to be ministered unto, but to minister, and to give his life a ransom for many" (Mark 10:45, KJV). When we pray, we align our hearts with Jesus' example, embracing the joy that comes from serving others as He did.

Furthermore, 1 Peter 4:10 encourages us to use our gifts to serve others: "As every man hath received the gift, even so minister the same one to another, as good stewards of the manifold grace of

God" (1 Peter 4:10, KJV). Prayer helps us to discern how we can use our unique talents and resources to serve others effectively, bringing glory to God and blessing those we serve.

Before moving forward, take a moment to pray: "Heavenly Father, I thank You for the opportunity to serve others in love. Help me to find joy in serving, knowing that I am following in the footsteps of Jesus. Guide me in using my gifts and talents to bless those around me, and give me the strength and compassion to serve selflessly. May my service be a reflection of Your love and grace, and may it bring glory to Your name. In Jesus' name, Amen."

Reflect on the areas in your life where you can serve others. How can you incorporate prayer into your acts of service? Consider asking God to show you specific ways to serve those around you and to give you a joyful heart as you serve.

Prayer is essential in finding joy in service because it helps us to see serving others as a way to express God's love and to grow in our faith. By making prayer a priority, you invite God to guide your service, ensuring that it is both meaningful and aligned with His will.

Notes

CHAPTER *Sixteen*

HEALING THROUGH PRAYER

ife can bring physical, emotional, and spiritual wounds that require healing. As a new adult, you may be dealing with past hurts, present struggles, or uncertainties about the future. Healing through prayer is a powerful way to invite God into your pain, trusting Him to restore and renew you. The Bible offers assurance of God's healing power in Psalm 147:3, "He healeth the broken in heart, and bindeth up their wounds" (Psalm 147:3, KJV). This verse reminds us that God is deeply compassionate and capable of healing even the most profound wounds.

Prayer is essential in the healing process because it allows us to bring our hurts to God, seeking His comfort and restoration. James 5:15 says, "And the prayer of faith shall save the sick, and the Lord shall raise him up; and if he have committed sins, they shall be forgiven him" (James 5:15, KJV). Through prayer, we can ask God to heal us physically, emotionally, and spiritually, trusting in His power and mercy.

Furthermore, Isaiah 53:5 points to the ultimate source of our healing: "But he was wounded for our transgressions, he was bruised for our iniquities: the chastisement of our peace was upon him; and with his stripes we are healed" (Isaiah 53:5, KJV). Jesus' sacrifice on the cross not only provides for our salvation but also for our healing. By bringing our pain to Him in prayer, we acknowledge His victory over sin and suffering, trusting that He will bring healing in His perfect timing.

Before moving forward, take a moment to pray: "Heavenly Father, I bring before You the wounds and struggles that weigh on my heart. I ask for Your healing touch to restore me physically, emotionally, and spiritually. Help me to trust in Your power to heal, and to find comfort in Your presence as I wait for Your perfect work in my life. Thank You for the sacrifice of Jesus, which provides the ultimate healing for my soul. I surrender my pain to You, Lord, and ask for Your peace to fill my heart. In Jesus' name, Amen."

Reflect on the areas of your life where you need healing. How can you invite God into these places through prayer? Consider setting aside time each day to pray specifically for healing, trusting that God hears your prayers and is at work even when you cannot see the immediate results.

Prayer is essential in the healing process because it connects us with God's love and power, allowing Him to work in our lives in profound ways. By making prayer a priority, you invite God to bring healing and restoration to your life, trusting that He is faithful to complete the work He has begun in you.

Notes

CHAPTER *Seventeen*
STRENGTHENING FAMILY BONDS

Family relationships are foundational to our lives, and as a new adult, you may be navigating the dynamics of these relationships in new ways. Strengthening family bonds through prayer is a powerful way to ensure that these relationships are rooted in love, understanding, and God's guidance. The Bible emphasizes the importance of family in Ephesians 6:1-2, "Children, obey your parents in the Lord: for this is right. Honour thy father and mother; which is the first commandment with promise" (Ephesians 6:1-2, KJV). This passage highlights the significance of respect and honor within the family, laying the groundwork for strong, healthy relationships.

Prayer plays a crucial role in fostering unity and love within families. Colossians 3:13 encourages us to "Forbear one another, and forgive one another, if any man have a quarrel against any: even as Christ forgave you, so also do ye" (Colossians 3:13, KJV). Through prayer, we can seek God's help in forgiving past hurts, being patient with one another, and maintaining harmony within our families.

Moreover, Proverbs 22:6 underscores the long-term impact of a strong family foundation: "Train up a child in the way he should go: and when he is old, he will not depart from it" (Proverbs 22:6, KJV). By praying for our families, we invest in the spiritual well-being of future generations, asking God to guide and protect our loved ones as they grow.

Before moving forward, take a moment to pray: "Heavenly Father, I thank You for the gift of family. I ask for Your guidance and strength to build and maintain strong, loving relationships within my family. Help me to be a source of love, patience, and forgiveness, reflecting Your grace in all my interactions. Strengthen the bonds between us, and guide us in Your truth, that we may honor You in all that we do. Protect our family, Lord, and help us to grow closer to one another and to You. In Jesus' name, Amen."

Reflect on your family relationships. How can you use prayer to strengthen these bonds? Consider praying specifically for each family member, asking God to bless them and to work in their lives, and for the unity and peace of your family as a whole.

Prayer is essential in strengthening family bonds because it invites God's love and wisdom into your relationships, fostering unity, understanding, and lasting connections. By making prayer a priority, you help to ensure that your family remains a source of strength and support, grounded in God's love and guidance.

Notes

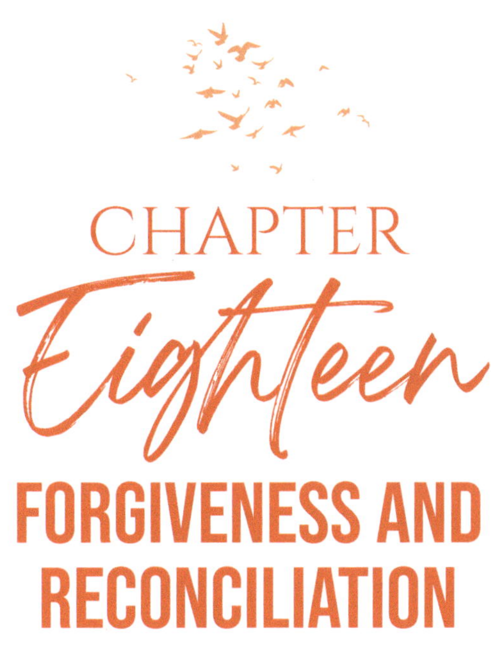

CHAPTER *Eighteen*

FORGIVENESS AND RECONCILIATION

orgiveness is one of the most challenging yet essential aspects of any relationship, and as a new adult, you may find yourself in situations where forgiveness and reconciliation are necessary. Holding onto grudges or unresolved conflicts can create barriers in your relationships and hinder your spiritual growth. The Bible calls us to forgive in Matthew 6:14-15, "For if ye forgive men their trespasses, your heavenly Father will also forgive you: But if ye forgive not men their trespasses, neither will your Father forgive your trespasses" (Matthew 6:14-15, KJV). This verse underscores the importance of forgiveness, not only for the sake of others but also for our own spiritual well-being.

Prayer is a powerful tool in the process of forgiveness. When we pray, we ask God to soften our hearts, to help us let go of anger and resentment, and to give us the strength to forgive those who have wronged us. Ephesians 4:31-32 encourages us, "Let all bitterness, and wrath, and anger, and clamour, and evil speaking, be put away from you, with all malice: And be ye kind one to another, tenderhearted, forgiving one another, even as God for Christ's sake hath forgiven you" (Ephesians 4:31-32, KJV). Through prayer, we can seek

God's help in cultivating a spirit of kindness and forgiveness, following His example.

Reconciliation, the restoration of relationships, is also a vital part of the healing process. Romans 12:18 advises, "If it be possible, as much as lieth in you, live peaceably with all men" (Romans 12:18, KJV). While reconciliation may not always be possible in every situation, prayer helps us to seek peace and to take the steps necessary to restore broken relationships where it is safe and healthy to do so.

Before moving forward, take a moment to pray: "Heavenly Father, I come before You with the hurts and grievances that weigh on my heart. I ask for Your strength to forgive those who have wronged me, just as You have forgiven me. Help me to let go of anger and bitterness, and to seek reconciliation where it is possible. Guide me in showing love and kindness, even in difficult situations, and give me the peace that comes from forgiving others. Thank You for Your grace and mercy, and for the example of forgiveness that You have set for me. In Jesus' name, Amen."

Reflect on any unresolved conflicts or hurts in your life. How can you bring these to God in prayer, seeking His help in forgiving and, if possible, reconciling with others? Consider reaching out to those you need to forgive, offering peace and seeking resolution where appropriate.

Prayer is essential in the process of forgiveness and reconciliation because it invites God's healing and grace into our hearts, enabling us to forgive others and restore broken relationships. By making prayer a priority, you allow God to work in your life, bringing about the peace and freedom that comes from true forgiveness.

Notes

CHAPTER
Nineteen
OVERCOMING TEMPTATION

Temptation is a challenge that everyone faces, and as a new adult, you may encounter various situations that test your values and faith. Overcoming temptation requires not only personal strength but also reliance on God's power and guidance. The Bible provides clear instruction on how to deal with temptation in 1 Corinthians 10:13, "There hath no temptation taken you but such as is common to man: but God is faithful, who will not suffer you to be tempted above that ye are able; but will with the temptation also make a way to escape, that ye may be able to bear it" (1 Corinthians 10:13, KJV). This verse assures us that God is always present, providing a way out of any tempting situation if we seek His help.

Prayer is a crucial element in overcoming temptation. Through prayer, we ask God for the strength to resist, the wisdom to recognize the dangers, and the guidance to choose the right path. Jesus Himself taught us to pray against temptation in Matthew 6:13, "And lead us not into temptation, but deliver us from evil" (Matthew 6:13, KJV). This prayer reflects our need for God's protection and deliverance from situations that could lead us astray.

Moreover, James 4:7 offers a powerful strategy for overcoming temptation: "Submit yourselves therefore to God. Resist the devil, and he will flee from you" (James 4:7, KJV). By submitting to God through prayer and obedience, we can resist the temptations that come our way, knowing that God's power is greater than any challenge we face.

Before moving forward, take a moment to pray: "Heavenly Father, I acknowledge that I am often faced with temptations that challenge my faith and values. I ask for Your strength and guidance to resist these temptations and to choose the path that honors You. Lead me away from situations that could lead me into sin, and help me to remain steadfast in my commitment to You. Thank You for always providing a way out and for being my source of strength in times of trial. In Jesus' name, Amen."

Reflect on the areas of your life where you are most vulnerable to temptation. How can you incorporate prayer into your daily routine to strengthen your resolve and seek God's guidance in those moments? Consider creating a prayer strategy that includes specific prayers for resisting temptation and staying focused on God's will.

Prayer is essential in overcoming temptation because it connects us with God's power and protection, enabling us to resist and overcome the challenges we face. By making prayer a priority, you equip yourself with the spiritual tools needed to stay strong in your faith and to live a life that reflects God's holiness.

Notes

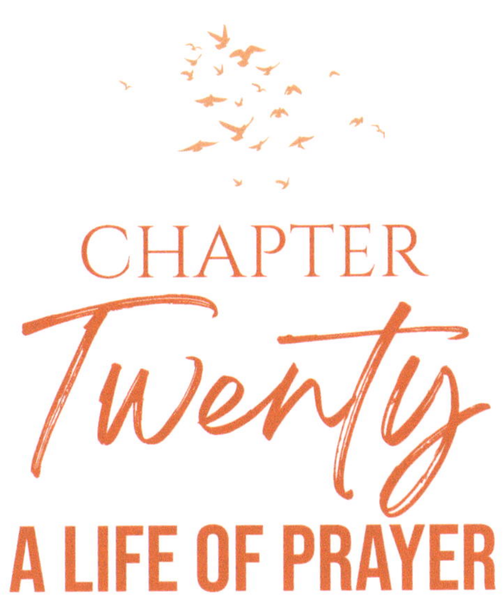

CHAPTER
Twenty
A LIFE OF PRAYER

As you journey through life, prayer will continue to be your most powerful and transformative tool. It is through prayer that you build and maintain your relationship with God, finding strength, guidance, and peace in every situation. The Bible encourages us in 1 Thessalonians 5:17 to "Pray without ceasing" (1 Thessalonians 5:17, KJV). This simple yet profound instruction highlights the importance of making prayer a continuous part of your daily life, not just during times of need but in every moment.

Living a life of prayer means acknowledging God's presence in all aspects of your life. Whether you are celebrating joys, facing challenges, or making decisions, prayer invites God into your experiences, allowing His wisdom and love to guide you. Philippians 4:6-7 reminds us, "Be careful for nothing; but in everything by prayer and supplication with thanksgiving let your requests be made known unto God. And the peace of God, which passeth all understanding, shall keep your hearts and minds through Christ Jesus" (Philippians 4:6-7, KJV). Through consistent prayer, you can experience the peace that comes from trusting God with every detail of your life.

As you continue to grow in your faith, remember that prayer is not just about asking for what you need but also about listening to God, giving thanks, and seeking His will. In Jeremiah 29:12-13, God promises, "Then shall ye call upon me, and ye shall go and pray unto me, and I will hearken unto you. And ye shall seek me, and find me, when ye shall search for me with all your heart" (Jeremiah 29:12-13, KJV). This promise assures us that when we earnestly seek God through prayer, He is faithful to listen and respond.

Before concluding, take a moment to pray: "Heavenly Father, I thank You for the gift of prayer and for the opportunity to grow closer to You through it. Help me to live a life of prayer, continuously seeking Your presence, wisdom, and guidance. May my relationship with You deepen as I make prayer a priority in all that I do. Lead me, strengthen me, and fill me with Your peace as I trust in Your unfailing love. Thank You for being my constant companion and for hearing my prayers. In Jesus' name, Amen."

Reflect on how you can incorporate prayer into every aspect of your life. How can you ensure that prayer remains a consistent and vital part of your daily routine? Consider setting specific times for prayer, developing a prayer journal, or joining a prayer group to keep your prayer life vibrant and strong.

A life of prayer is a life lived in close communion with God. By making prayer a priority, you open the door for God to work powerfully in your life, guiding, comforting, and transforming you as you walk with Him. As you move forward in your journey, may prayer continue to be the foundation upon which you build your faith, your decisions, and your relationships, trusting in God's goodness and grace every step of the way.

Notes